W9-AUJ-763

TANTALIZING MAZES

Dave Phillips

Dover Publications, Inc., New York

Introduction

Here is a collection of 36 challenging and amusing mazes that look easy at first glance, but have various complications that are sure to test your maze-solving skills. These puzzles have a wide range of objectives, restrictions and routes. In one maze you have to eat your way through various slices of pizza, in another you are to gather up eight pieces of scrap paper and bring them to a wastebasket before exiting the maze.

These intriguing puzzles are small enough so that perseverance alone will eventually succeed, but you'll find them more rewarding if you use your ingenuity and your maze-solving sense. If, for whatever reason, you find a maze impossible to work out, you may refer to the solutions on pages 37 to 45.

Copyright © 1992 by Dave Phillips.
All rights reserved under Pan American and International Copyright Conventions.

Published in Canada by General Publishing Company, Ltd., 30 Lesmill Road, Don Mills, Toronto, Ontario.

Published in the United Kingdom by Constable and Company, Ltd., 3 The Lanchesters, 162–164 Fulham Palace Road, London W6 9ER.

Tantalizing Mazes is a new work, first published by Dover Publications, Inc., in 1992.

Manufactured in the United States of America
Dover Publications, Inc., 31 East 2nd Street, Mineola, N.Y. 11501

Library of Congress Cataloging-in-Publication Data

Phillips, Dave.
    Tantalizing mazes / Dave Phillips.
        p.   cm.
    ISBN 0-486-27097-1
    1. Maze puzzles. I. Title.
GV1507.M3P48 1992
793.73—dc20
                                                                            91-42183
                                                                            CIP

Strawberries and Cream.

Find a path that passes through three strawberries and ends up in the cream, then find another path that passes through the remaining three strawberries and also ends in the cream. You may not use any part of a path more than once.

1

Blizzard.

Find a path that enters the maze, passes through all snowflakes, and exits the maze, without using any part of a path more than once. Note that there are three shapes of snowflakes. The order of the first three flakes you pass through must be followed throughout the maze.

Rainy Days.

Find a path that runs through all umbrellas, rain clouds and the sun, and,
without having used any part of a path more than once, exits the maze.
From an umbrella you must go to a rain cloud.

Jacks.

Find a path that enters the maze, passes through all jacks and the two balls, and exits the maze, without using any part of a path more than once. You must collect four jacks before passing through the first ball, and then five jacks before passing through the second ball.

Wastebasket.

Find a path that enters the maze, passes through all paper and then the wastebasket, and exits the maze, without using any part of a path more than once.

Chips and Dip.

Find six separate paths that enter the maze, pass through a chip, and end in the dip. Then find a path from the dip out of the maze. You may not use any part of a path more than once.

Seven Elves.

Find a path that enters the maze, passes through all elves, and exits the maze, without using any path more than once. You may not go from one elf to another unless there are differences between at least three elements of their appearance.

Cats and Mice.

Find a path that enters the maze, goes through all cats, all mice and the dog, and exits the maze, without using any part of a path more than once. A mouse may not go to a cat and a cat may not go to the dog.

Spiderweb.

Find a path that starts at the spider, passes through all flies, and ends back at the spider, without using any part of a path more than once. You may not pass through the same kind of fly twice in a row.

Two Dozen Doughnuts.

Find a path that enters the maze, passes through all doughnuts, and exits the maze, without using any part of a path more than once. You must have three of each kind of doughnut in the first dozen and in the second dozen as well.

10

Pepperoni Pizza.

Find a path that enters the maze, advances through all pizza sections, and exits the maze, without using any part of a path more than once. First pass through a whole slice, then a half-eaten one, and then a crust. Repeat this order two more times.

Sand Castles.

Find a path that enters the maze, passes through all spades, buckets and castles, and exits the maze, without using any part of a path more than once. The order *spade, bucket, castle* must be followed throughout the maze.

Monkeys and Bananas.

Find a path that enters the maze, passes through all monkeys and bananas, and exits the maze, without using any part of a path more than once. You must go through two bananas before passing through a monkey.

Clowns.

Find a path that enters the maze, travels through all clowns, and exits the maze, without using any part of a path more than once. You may not pass through the same kind of clown twice in a row.

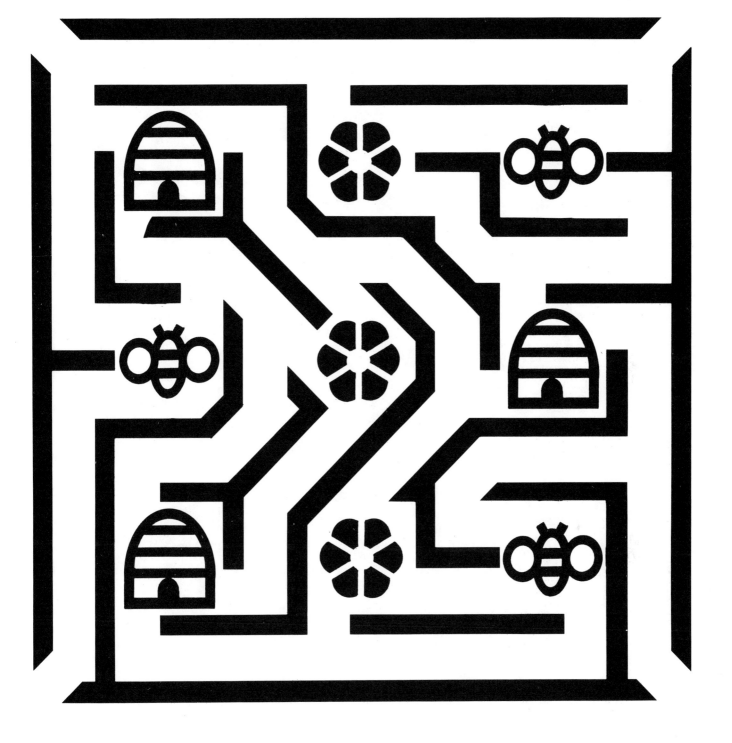

Beehive.

Find a path that enters the maze, passes through all bees, hives and flowers, and exits the maze. Do not use any part of a path more than once. You must stick to this order: bee to flower to hive.

Popcorn.

Find a path that enters the maze, passes through all popcorn, and the two mouths, and exits the maze, without using any part of a path more than once. You must collect three popped kernels before passing through a mouth.

Peanuts.

Find a path that enters the maze, passes through all peanuts, both squirrels and the elephant, and exits the maze, without using any part of a path more than once. You must collect one peanut before going to a squirrel and four peanuts in a row for the elephant.

Donkeys and Carrots.

Find a path that enters the maze, continues on through all carrots and donkeys, and exits the maze, without using any part of a path more than once. You must collect two carrots before going to each donkey.

Dog Biscuits.

Find a path that enters the maze, passes through all dog biscuits and the two dogs, and exits the maze, without using any part of a path more than once. You must collect four biscuits prior to meeting each dog.

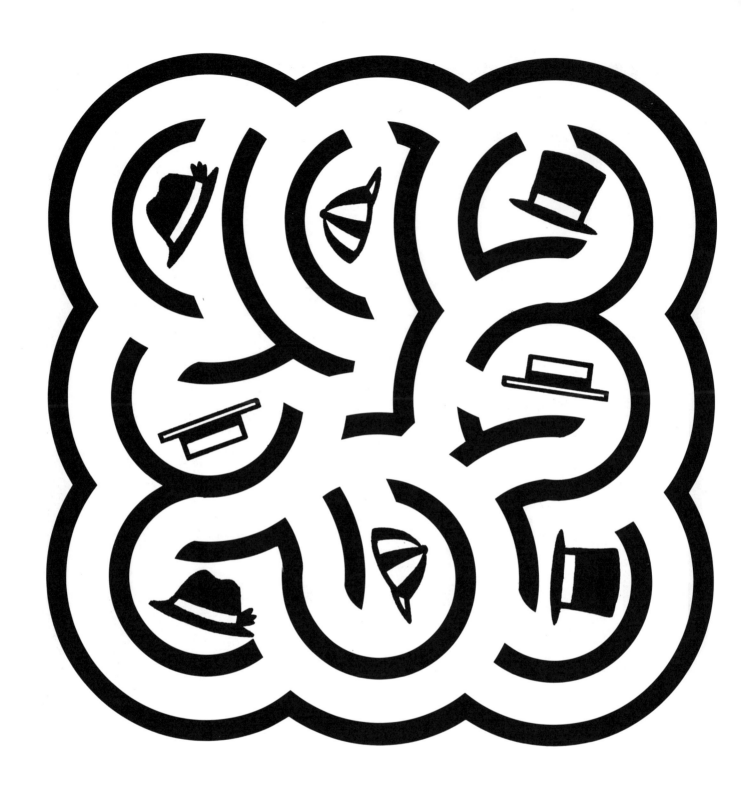

Hats Off.

Find four separate paths that connect each hat to its twin. You must not use any part of a path more than once.

Lighthouse.

Find a path that leads each boat out of the maze, and a path that enters the maze and ends at the lighthouse. In the course of these trips, you must also pass over each buoy once. You may not use any part of a path more than once.

Tennis.

Find a path that enters the maze, passes through all tennis rackets, and exits the maze, without using any part of a path more than once. You must cross over the net after passing through each racket.

Corn on the Cob.

Find a path that enters the maze, passes through all corn and both hungry guys, and exits the maze, without using any part of a path more than once. You must pass through three corncobs before passing through a hungry guy.

Tossed Salad.

Find a path that enters the maze, passes through the whole salad, and exits the maze, without using any part of a path more than once. You may not pass through the same ingredient three times in a row.

Good and Bad.

Find a path that enters the maze, proceeds through all devils and angels, and exits the maze, without using any part of a path more than once. You must alternate between devils and angels.

Roundup.

Find a path that enters the maze, passes through all horses, and exits the maze, without using any part of a path more than once. You must collect horses in same-color pairs.

Horn Section.

Find two separate paths (without using any part of a path more than once) that enter the maze, pass through one half of the horns, and exit the maze. Each path must collect two of each kind of horn.

Dragon Quest.

Find a path that enters the maze, passes through all swords and ends at the dragon, without using any part of a path more than once. You may only pass over a sword hilt-first.

Bat Cave.

Find a path that enters the maze, travels through all bats, torches and the treasure, and exits the maze, without using any part of a path more than once. You must pass through a torch before moving through a bat.

Halloween.

Find two separate paths that enter the maze and end at the pumpkin in the center. One path must collect all the skulls, the other all the ghosts. Do not use any part of a path more than once.

Iced Tea.

Find a path that enters the maze, runs through all lemons, straws and tea, and exits the maze, without using any part of a path more than once. You must use the order: *tea, straw, lemon*.

Jolly Roger.

Find a path that enters the maze, passes through all pirates, knives and the Jolly Roger (the pirate flag), and exits the maze, without using any part of a path more than once. A pirate must go to a knife, but only meeting it hilt-first.

Hat Trick.

Find a path that starts at the star, passes through all hats, all rabbits and wands, and exits the maze, without using any part of a path more than once. You must proceed in the order: wand to hat and then three rabbits.

Square Peg, Round Hole.

Find a path that enters the maze, goes through all pegs and holes, and exits the maze, without using any part of a path more than once. A round peg must go to a round hole and a square peg to a square hole.

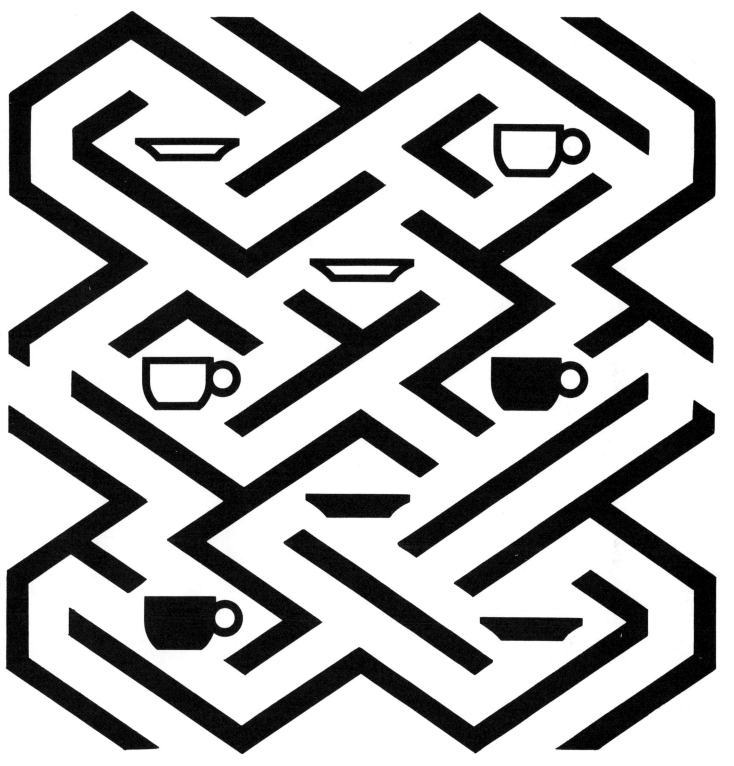

Tea Party.

Find a path that enters the maze, passes through all cups and saucers, and exits the maze, without using any part of a path more than once. A black cup must go to a black saucer and a white cup must go to a white saucer.

Lizards.

Find a path that enters the maze, passes through all lizards, and exits the maze, without using any part of a path more than once. You may not enter a lizard's chamber by way of its mouth.

Solutions

Strawberries and Cream, page 1

Blizzard, page 2

Rainy Days, page 3

Jacks, page 4

Wastebasket, page 5

Chips and Dip, page 6

Seven Elves, page 7

Cats and Mice, page 8

Spiderweb, page 9

Two Dozen Doughnuts, page 10

Pepperoni Pizza, page 11

Sand Castles, page 12

Monkeys and Bananas, page 13

Clowns, page 14

Beehive, page 15

Popcorn, page 16

Peanuts, page 17

Donkeys and Carrots, page 18

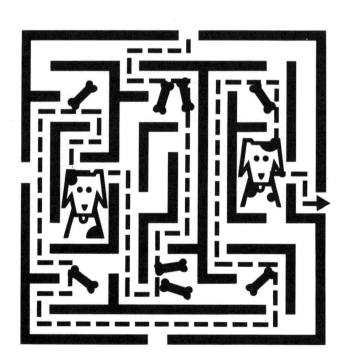

Dog Biscuits, page 19

Hats Off, page 20

Lighthouse, page 21

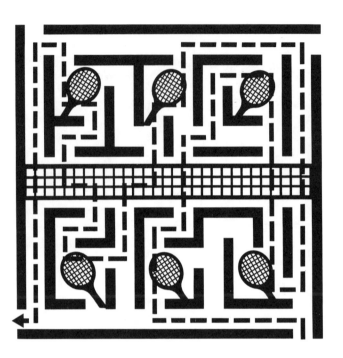

Tennis, page 22

Corn on the Cob, page 23

Tossed Salad, page 24

Good and Bad, page 25

Roundup, page 26

Horn Section, page 27

Dragon Quest, page 28

Bat Cave, page 29

Halloween, page 30

Iced Tea, page 31

Jolly Roger, page 32

Hat Trick, page 33

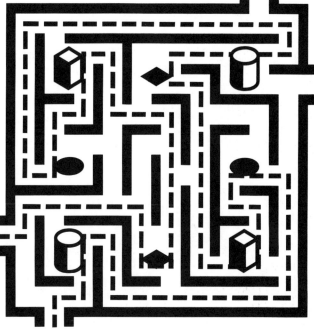

Square Peg, Round Hole, page 34

Tea Party, page 35

Lizards, page 36